A WORD IN THE HAND

BOOK 1

Written by Jane L. Kitterman
and S. Harold Collins

Illustrated by
Alison McKinley

A Breath of Fresh Air
GarlicPress

Published by
Garlic Press
605 Powers
Eugene, OR 97402

Reorder No. GP-042

www.garlicpress.com

TABLE OF CONTENTS

PREFACE

We have written *A WORD IN THE HAND: An Introduction to Sign Language* for sign language instructors in two distinctive settings, the classroom and community education. Both settings are fertile for teaching sign language.

Classroom instructors will find that signing is an approach to language and English in a novel way. While children are learning to talk with their hands, they must do so in conformity to the tense, vocabulary, word usage, and syntactical patterns of standard English.

We have often observed that learners whose spelling, writing, or other communication skills are low respond unexpectedly to this new medium of expression.

In addition, learners will benefit from an introduction to a handicapping condition. Perhaps their sensitivity to a hearing impairment will carry over into other limiting human conditions—blindness, retardation, learning difficulties, or physical impairments.

Community education, whether sponsored by governmental bodies or initiated by like-minded individuals, is the second setting in which *A WORD IN THE HAND* will appeal.

People who attend sign language offerings in community settings do so for widely different reasons. Typical reasons are: a desire to communicate with deaf relatives, friends, or co-workers; a need by care professionals and public employees (fire and police personnel and teachers) to have a simple competency should they encounter a signing person; and a need for people with speech or hearing problems to increase their communications skills.

LESSON FORMAT

The fifteen lessons in *A WORD IN THE HAND* are written in a standard teaching procedure, lessons have: a skills game, a review, new vocabulary, practice, and an assignment. Each lesson allows the instructor to choose the presentation material which best conforms to student capabilities and available teaching time. With this approach, each lesson can be used for a single presentation or spread over several sessions.

PRESENTATION OF VOCABULARY

A formal vocabulary of 480 plus words is presented in fifteen lessons. With the addition of the past tense and the endings of -ly, *-ing, -y,* and -s, the size of the vocabulary will be significantly more.

Signs sometimes vary due to locality or dominant choice. We have tried to use the easiest or most common sign for our vocabulary words.

Each lesson lists words by category, most commonly by parts of speech— i.e., nouns, verbs, adjectives. Please remember that some words can be used for more than one category. For instance, some nouns can also be used as verbs. When word categories change and when that change requires a different sign, we have so indicated—an example is the sign for the noun 'color' and the sign for the verb 'color'.

Vocabulary is sequential. New lessons use past vocabulary. But recognizing a need for flexibility, an instructor can jump ahead to acquire a needed vocabulary if they remember to modify appropriately that advanced lesson in accord with what has been taught. An instructor may want to teach Lesson 15 on CLOTHES after Lesson 3 on PEOPLE. That is possible if the sentences in Part E of Lesson 15 are revamped to include the vocabulary, tense, and syntactics comparable to Lesson 3.

We hope that you find the signed vocabulary clear. It has been drawn to provide the visual emphasis so necessary to remembering.

AN ADDED RESOURCE

We highly recommend the materials published by Gallaudet University Press as resources or embellishments to this book. For information on deaf education and publications for the hearing impaired, write to Gallaudet University, 7th and Florida Avenue, N.E., Washington, D.C., 20002.

1 INTRODUCTION

BACKGROUND & HISTORY

1. A Brief Perspective: Teaching the Deaf
2. A Brief Background: Hearing Impairments
3. Educating the Hearing Impaired Today

INTRODUCE THE ALPHABET

1. The Finger Spelling Alphabet is basic to all signing.
   a. When signs are unknown or do not exist, precise spelling is used.
2. Go slowly through the alphabet.
   a. Review at intervals.
   b. Provide associations for signs that are difficult to remember.
   c. Students should be forming the letters as they are presented.
3. Form letters and future words—with clean motions and in an area between lip and shoulder height.

PRACTICE THE ALPHABET

Practice putting letters together when the alphabet is firm.

1. Randomly sign one letter for identification.
2. Combine two letters for identification.
3. Combine three letters for simple words.
   a. Double letters, as in 'bee', are easily indicated by bouncing the signing hand to accent each letter.
4. "What Comes Next?" Sign two consecutive letters (for instance: g, h). Students sign the following two letters (i, j).
5. Name a letter to which students respond by forming the signs.
6. Spell the first three letters of a child's name. That child finishes their name.
7. "The Alphabet Song" for young children sing, "A, B, C, D, E, F, G, H, 1, J, K, L, M, N, O, P, Q, R, S, T, U, V, W, X, Y, Z, Now I know my ABC's, what do you think of me?" Sign the letters as you sing the song.

(OPT.) INTRODUCE NUMBERS 1 TO 20

A BRIEF PERSPECTIVE: TEACHING THE DEAF

Sign language did not emerge as a formal method of communicating until the sixteenth century. It was not until this era that people began to challenge the often held myths of deaf people as uneducable. The deaf to this time were considered variously as: incapable of reasoning, possessed by satan, or incapable of living on their own. As such, they were generally dismissed as active participants in most social structures and settings.

As these myths were challenged, dedicated people worked to provide assistance to the deaf. In Italy, a physician, Girolamo Cardano, devised a code for teaching deaf people. In Spain, a monk, Pedro Ponce de Leon, succeeded in educating the deaf children of noble Spanish families. And soon a one-handed manual alphabet was devised by Juan Martin Pablo Bonet who also wrote and published a book extolling this alphabet.

Despite these pioneers, education of the deaf was limited to deaf individuals from wealthy or noble families.

It was in France and Germany that public education for deaf children began. In France, Abbe Charles l'Epee developed and refined a sign language that is the basis for signing today. In his public school, l'Epee educated deaf children in this *natural language* of signs, providing a strong model for a manual language and an education method that has been influential to this day.

In Germany, a second educational method arose. Samuel Henlke believed that deaf people could be educated through speechreading alone. His efforts lead to the *oral* method of educating the deaf.

In the United States, education of the deaf was most notably influenced by Thomas Hopkins Gallaudet. A minister, Gallaudet became interested in the deaf after being approached by a wealthy doctor whose daughter was deaf. Gallaudet subsequently gained training in France and later founded, in Hartford, Connecticut, the first U.S. school for the deaf.

A BRIEF BACKGROUND: HEARING IMPAIRMENTS

Hearing Impairment is a general description noting a problem with hearing. Impairments can be the result of hereditary traits. They can be the result of damage to the middle ear—the three tiny bones of the hammer, anvil, and stirrup—or to the inner ear—the auditory nerve and cochlea. Perhaps the most common impairment is simply the result of the human aging process.

Damage to the inner and middle ear can occur before, during, or after birth. Before birth intra-uteral diseases like rubella (measles), or venereal diseases can affect fetal development and hearing. Lack of maternal nutrition during pregnancy or injury to the mother during pregnancy can also affect hearing prior to birth.

During the birthing process, a premature delivery or a difficult delivery can impair the hearing of a child. After birth, complications, resulting from ear infections, fever, childhood diseases, and nutrition also cause hearing impairments.

Hearing impairments vary. Some people can hear more than others. Impairments can be measured by decibel and frequency losses. Decibels are a measure of loudness: a loss of 15 db – 50 db is considered mild; 50 db – 70 db moderate; 70 db – 90 db severe; and, a loss above 90 db is profound.

As a reference, most sounds range in the 30 db (a whisper) to 80 db (traffic) range, with casual conversation in the 40 – 50 db range. Working situations where noise is prominent often require ear plugs or protection when noise exceeds 90 db. Constant exposure to noise over 90 db (rock music, 110 db; jet planes, 120 db) can impair hearing.

A frequency loss also measures hearing impairment. Frequency is the pitch of a sound. Together, frequency and decibel loss give an accurate indication of hearing.

Most hearing impaired people wear hearing aids. Hearing aids do not automatically restore lost hearing. Aids help to amplify sound which in many cases increases the reception of sounds for the impaired person. Damage which has occurred to the auditory nerve, unfortunately, can not be simply corrected.

You might approach private and public agencies to borrow hearing aid models— eyeglasses, behind-the-ear aids, in-the-ear aids, or body aids. Familiarizing those not experiencing a hearing loss with devices their impaired peers use is valuable.

EDUCATING THE HEARING IMPAIRED TODAY

To better understand about sound, hearing, and hearing lose, consult our offering Sound Hearing, which is a audio tape and a booklet. The listener will hear as an impaired person might, while listening to music, a story, and taking a simple spelling test.

Two rivaling methods compete to educate the hearing impaired today. The oral approach teaches the impaired to use their residual hearing, to develop speech reading (lip reading), and to use visual and setting clues to assist hearing. Speech training is also used to develop voice quality and articulation of voiced sounds. Signing is not used.

Total communication provides much the same training, but includes signing as the major communication form. Signing has numerous variations, but two dominate. Forms of Signed English follow the syntactic and grammatical rules of the English language. American Sign Language (ASL), considered an actual language, has its own sentence structure, grammatical rules, and semantics.

To accent the two signing approaches, here are two sentences as signed according to each system:

> A Signed English person would sign: "I have a pretty new red coat."
>
> An ASL person would sign: "Coat my new pretty red."
>
> Signed English: "I will go to town tonight."
>
> ASL: "Me town go night."

Variations of Signed English are used largely in educational institutions preparing impaired children to read, write, and function by rules that apply to the hearing world. ASL is largely used by impaired people among themselves.

In this book, Signed English affords the grammar and sentence structure that hearing people use. It is much easier to teach Signed English patterned after the English language, than to teach a new language which, although it has a familiar vocabulary, varies in syntax and grammatical construction.

INTRODUCE THE ALPHABET

2 COLORS

REVIEW FINGER ALPHABET

1. Review single letters, or use suggestions from Lesson 1.
2. Game—adapt to students' level.
   a. Categories

   Signer states a category—for example, 'animals.' Then finger spells something from that category—'mouse'. Signer chooses a person to answer from raised hands. Correct answer allows that person to state next category and to finger spell.
   b. Names

   Sign a student's name. That student answers by saying their name aloud. Signer can remain leader, or signer can change with each person.

INTRODUCE NEW SIGNS

Special Note—**Past Tense Sign Markers**

Vocabulary list verbs are given only in the present tense (Lessons 2, 3 and 4 are the exception). Regular past tense verbs ending in **ed** are indicated by: (1.) signing the present tense, and immediately (2.) signing a **d**.

Verb + signed **d** = regular **ed** past tense; painted, colored, wanted, helped.

Colors	Pronouns	Articles	Verbs
black	I	a	1. Regular past
blue	you	the	tense **-ed**.
brown	your		color (colored)
green	me	**Conjunctions**	help (helped)
orange	it	and	paint (painted)
pink		but	want (wanted)
purple	**Adjectives**		2. Irregular
red	beautiful	**Common Words/**	past tense
white	big	**Phrases**	draw (drew)
yellow	little	yes	
color	some	no	
		please	
		thank you	

GAME

1. "**What color is**…" State or point to a colored object. Students respond with the sign.
2. Provide students with a worksheet that contains a number of objects. Ask the students to color, for example, the apple…(give a color sign).

SENTENCES

Be able to sign these sentences. Remember: **boldface** words need an **-ed** marker. Finger spell words not known.

1. I want a purple crayon.
2. Please help me paint a big house.
3. Draw a yellow sun.
4. Paint a purple pig.
5. Help me draw a green tree.
6. You **painted** a beautiful blue sky.
7. I want some candy.
8. Thank you for the brown paint.
9. I **wanted** green. You **wanted** black and orange.

ASSIGNMENT POSSIBILITIES

1. Be able to sign sentences in Part D.
2. Make up one (or more) sentence to sign next lesson. Finger spell signs not known.

VOCABULARY

a

and

beautiful

big

black

blue (D.M.)

brown

but

color (n)

color (v) (M.M.)

draw

green (D.M.)

(D.M.)—Double Movement   (M.M.)—Multiple Movement

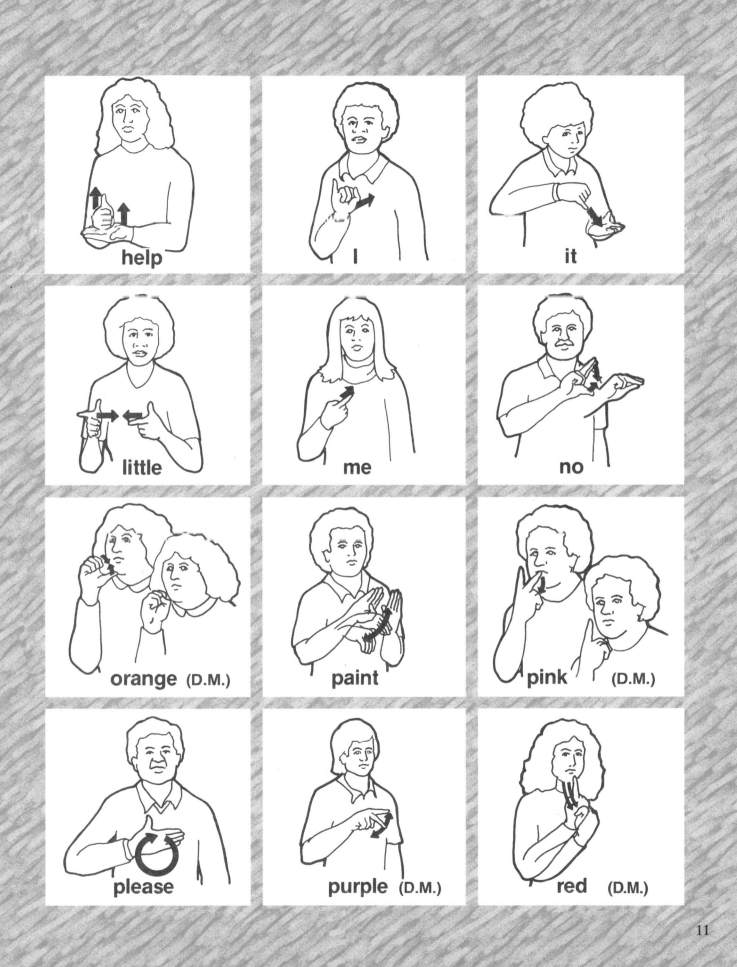

help

I

it

little

me

no

orange (D.M.)

paint

pink (D.M.)

please

purple (D.M.)

red (D.M.)

11

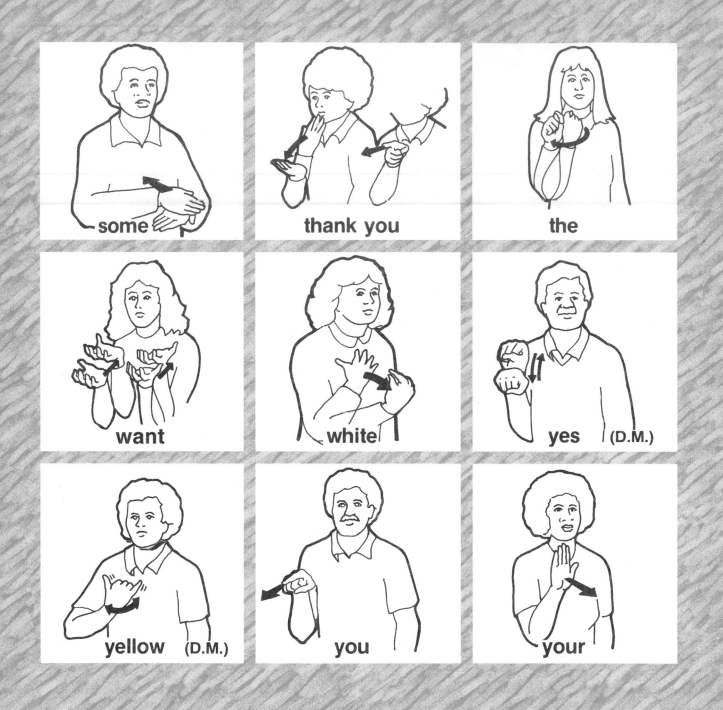

some

thank you

the

want

white

yes (D.M.)

yellow (D.M.)

you

your

3 PEOPLE

REVIEW

1. Lesson 2 Vocabulary.
2. Sign sentences from Part D, Lesson 2.
3. Sign homework sentences.
   One student signs their created sentence. They then call upon another student to interpret.

INTRODUCE NEW SIGNS

Special Notes:

Past Tense Sign Markers. Irregular past tense verbs do not end in **ed**. Past tense in the irregular case is indicated by: (1.) signing the present tense, and immediately (2.) motioning over the shoulder, like this:

Plural Sign Markers. Nouns from the Vocabulary are given in singular form (one). Make all nouns plural (more than one) by: (1.) signing the singular noun, and immediately (2.) adding an **s**. Verbs like **run** become **runs** in a similar manner.

Nouns	Pronouns	Articles	2. Irregular
boy	he	that	come (came)
brother	his	this	do (did)
children	him		run (ran)
family	she	**Prepositions**	sit (sat)
father	her	in	sleep (slept)
friend		to	3. Auxiliary
girl	**Adjectives**	under	am
man	tall	with	is
mother			are
people	**Adverbs**	**Verbs**	be
sister	fast	1. Regular	do
woman	slow	love (loved)	did
home		play (played)	was
house		visit (visited)	were
chair		walk (walked)	

EXERCISES & GAMES

1. Go over vocabulary words twice.
2. Students can practice in small groups.
3. Sign words to students. Students tell what they are.
4. Game:
    Have students write a short sentence on a piece of paper.
    Leader starts by signing their sentence.
    Leader calls upon another to interpret.
    The correct interpreter signs their sentence.

SENTENCES

Boldface words need a marker. Finger spell signs not known.

1. The girl **painted** a blue house.
2. The **boys ran** home from school.
3. That girl is tall.
4. The man **sat** in the purple chair.
5. That woman is beautiful.
6. The school is **painted** blue.
7. The **boys walked** home.

8. The baby **sleeps** in the house.
9. The boy and girl **played** in the house.
10. Please help me paint.
11. She **wants** to play with you.
12. He **sat** under the **chairs**.
13. He **sat** in the yellow chair.
14. The girl is under the house.
15. My family is home.
16. My friend **came** to visit me.

ASSIGNMENT POSSIBILITIES

1. Be able to sign the sentences in Part D.
2. Make up a two sentence short story.

VOCABULARY

am

are

be

boy

brother

chair

children (M.M.)

come

do (D.M.)

do

did

family

(D.M.)—Double Movement   (M.M.)—Multiple Movement

17

fast

father

friend

girl

he

her

him

his

home

house

in

is

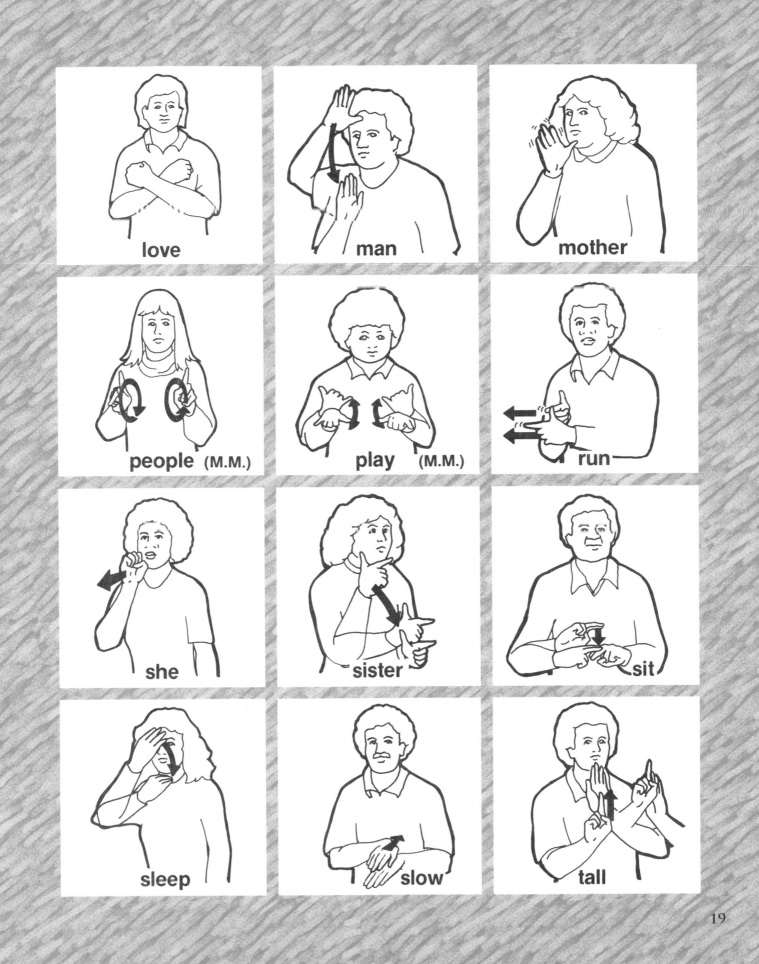

love

man

mother

people (M.M.)

play (M.M.)

run

she

sister

sit

sleep

slow

tall

that this to

under visit (M.M.) walk (M.M.)

was were with

woman

4 SCHOOL

FINGER SPELLING GAME

1. **Opposites**
Leader signs simple words—five letters or less. Students interpret finger spelling. A chosen student states the word finger spelled, then finger spells its opposite. Keep it simple, words like: day, up, tall, left, slow, cold, etc.

2. **For Younger Children**
Sign children's name, or simple letter combinations.

REVIEW

1. Signs from Lessons 2 and 3.
2. Sentences from Part D, Lesson 3.
3. Sign homework short stories.

INTRODUCE NEW SIGNS

Special Note: **-ing Marker.**

Add **-ing** to words by: (1.) signing the base word and immediately (2.) using this

Nouns	story	2. Irregular	**Adverbs**
bathroom	swing	break (broke)	very
book	tape	find (found)	
crayon	teacher	get (got)	**Propositions**
desk	time	go (gone)	at
glue		read (read)	on
name	**Verbs**	write (wrote)	
paper	1. Regular	3. Auxiliary	**Question Words**
pencil	climb (climbed)	can	what
school	jump (jumped)	will	where
scissors			who
slide			

EXERCISES

1. Go over vocabulary words twice.
2. Students can practice in small groups.
3. Sign words to students. Students tell what they are.

SENTENCES

Boldface words need a marker. Finger spell signs not known.

1. What color is your paper?
2. David **walked** to school.
3. The children **played** on the swing and slide.
4. Get your scissors and glue.
5. Write your name with your pencil.
6. Where are the **pencils**?
7. The **boys** love to climb and jump.
8. I am **going** to read and write at school.
9. Story time! Get me the book, please.
10. Who has the tape?
11. I want to go to the bathroom.
12. Kathy and Lori like **running** and **jumping**.
13. Can I have some paper, please?
14. What are the **names** of your **teachers**?
15. Go sit at your desk.

ASSIGNMENT POSSIBILITIES

1. Be able to sign the sentences from Part E.
2. Complete these sentences. Be able to sign or finger spell them:
   My name is _____.
   I go to _____ School. (Or, I work at _____.)
   I have _____ brothers and/or sisters.
   I like the colors _____ and _____.

VOCABULARY

at

bathroom

book

break

can

climb

crayon

desk

find

get

go

glue

(D.M.)—Double Movement   (M.M.)—Multiple Movement

24

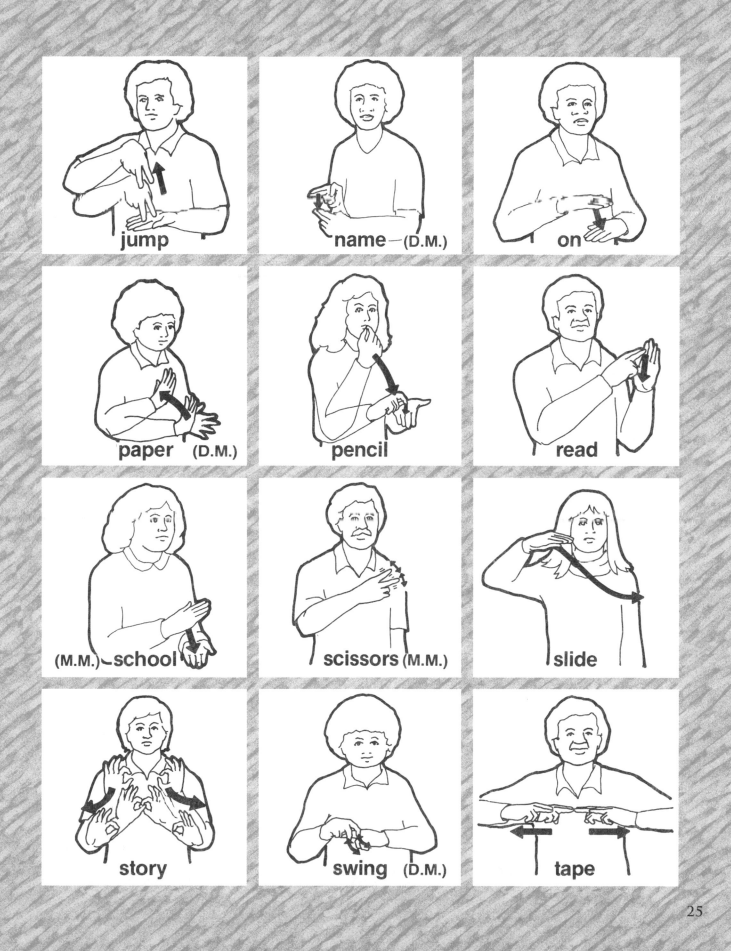

jump

name (D.M.)

on

paper (D.M.)

pencil

read

(M.M.) school

scissors (M.M.)

slide

story

swing (D.M.)

tape

25

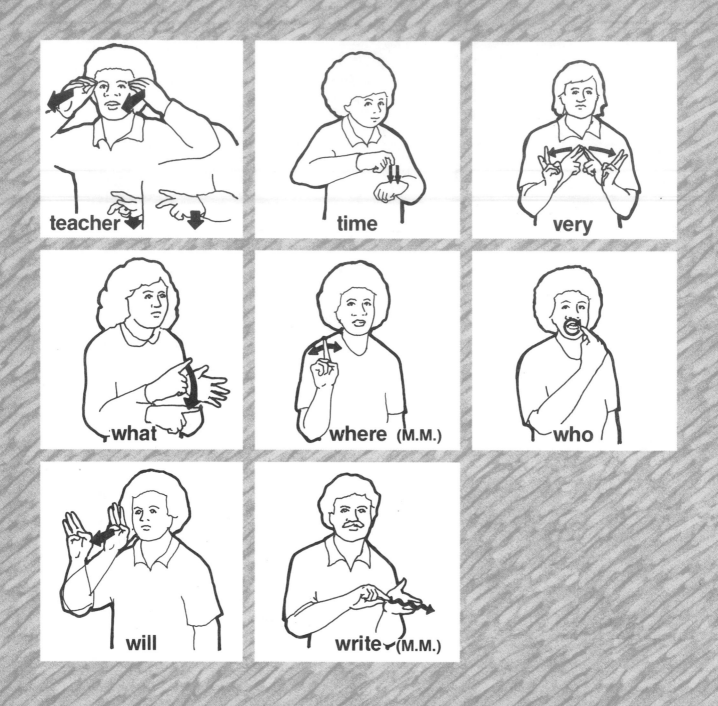

teacher

time

very

what

where (M.M.)

who

will

write (M.M.)

5 HOME

FINGER SPELLING GAME

(Choose One)

1. Rhyming I

Leader prepares a list, or students can provide words. Sign a word. A chosen student says the word and signs a word that rhymes. Sign 'coat.' "Coat," sign 'float.' All students can be asked what the rhyming word is, or the signer can say it after signing it.

2. Rhyming II

Leader prepares a list and uses this presentation pattern: "My word rhymes with (finger spell). It is …"

My word rhymes with:		
(ink)	It is a color.	(pink)
(rat)	It is soft and likes milk.	(cat)
(four)	It is something we walk on.	(floor)
(fire)	It is something a car has.	(tire)
(scale)	It is a weather condition.	(hail)

Chosen students respond by finger spelling and saying their guess. Leader indicates correctness.

REVIEW

1. Lesson 4 signs and any other signs that have proven difficult.
2. Sign sentences from Part E, Lesson 4.
3. On the Spot Signing:
   Have all or selected children *quickly* make up a sentence to be signed to all.
4. Share homework assignments from Lesson 4.
5. Review **past tense verbs**. How would you sign:

came	drew	walked	wrote
sat	ran	visited	loved
played	got	jumped	read
helped	went	broke	climbed

6. Review **-ing markers**. How would you sign:

loving	painting	running	drawing
coloring	wanting	writing	sleeping
getting	coming	reading	visiting
going	sitting	breaking	playing

INTRODUCE NEW SIGNS

Nouns		Verbs	Adjectives
room	cup	**1. Regular**	clean
bedroom	fork	close	dirty
kitchen	glass	look	many
livingroom	plate	need	new
bathtub	spoon	open	old
refrigerator	clock	wash	
sink	couch	watch	**Adverbs-**
stove	door	**2. Irregular**	**Prepositions**
table	light	put	out
toilet	television	**3. Auxiliary**	up
	telephone	have	down
	water	has	
		had	

EXERCISES

1. Go over vocabulary words twice.
2. Students can practice in small groups.
3. Sign words to students. Students tell what they are.

SENTENCES

1. Put the chair in the kitchen, please.
2. Help me wash the cups.
3. Your new bed is in your room.
4. Clean the livingroom.
5. The kitchen door is open. Please close it.
6. We have a new television and couch.
7. Can you come and watch television at my house?
8. Turn the water on in the sink. Thank you.
9. The refrigerator is big and it is white.
10. Time to eat. Put the plates, forks, spoons, and glasses on the table.
11. The bathroom is dirty, please clean it.
12. We are getting new chairs for the bedroom.
13. That house is old.
14. We have many telephones.
15. Walk to the bedroom.

ASSIGNMENT POSSIBILITIES

1. Be prepared to sign the sentences from Part E.
2. Be prepared to sign an event, occasion, or something significant that happened to you recently.

VOCABULARY

bathtub

bedroom

clean

clock

close

couch

cup

dirty (M.M.)

door

down

fork

glass

(D.M.)—Double Movement   (M.M.)—Multiple Movement

31

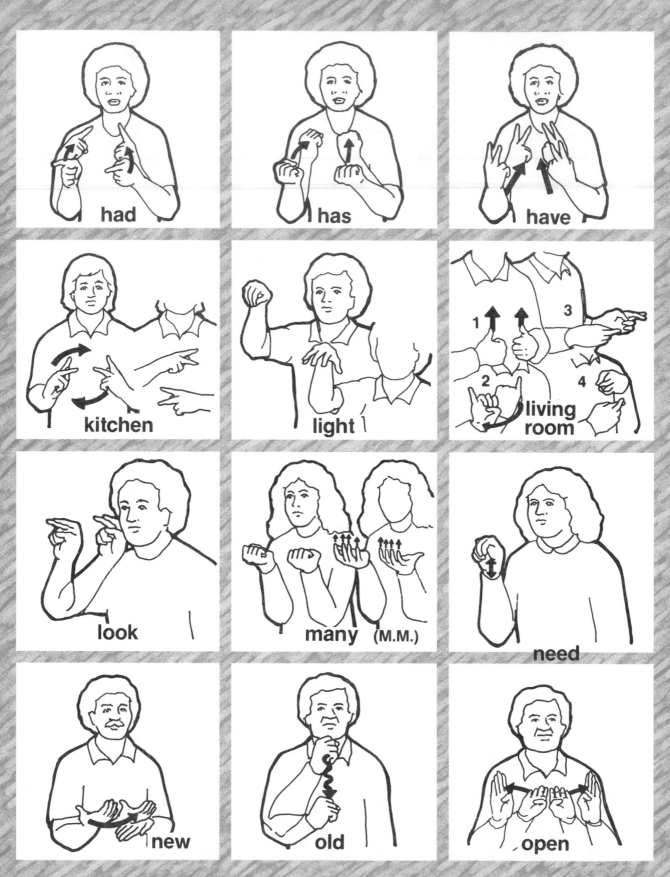

had

has

have

kitchen

light

living room

1 2 3 4

look

many (M.M.)

need

new

old

open

out

plate

put

refrigerator (M.M.)

room

sink

spoon

stove

table

telephone

television

toilet (M.M.)

33

up

wash (M.M.)

watch

watch

water

6 ACTIVITIES, TOYS & GAMES

FINGER SPELLING GAME

(Choose One)

1. **Things Found in A Store.**
   Leader tells what kind of store their object can be found in—grocery, department, shoe, appliance store. The chosen object is finger spelled. Leader calls on a raised hand. Correct answer spells the next object.

2. **26 Words.**
   Leader must prepare a list of 26 words, one for each letter in the alphabet. Words should be appropriate to the students' understanding—three letter words serve well.
   Students letter paper A to Z.
   Leader randomly signs a word. Students write the signed letters next to the A to Z letter that begins the word. Words are signed twice.
   Once complete, read back all 26 words. Who got all or most correct?

REVIEW

1. Review signs from Lesson 5, plus any other signs that have persisted as difficult from other lessons.
2. Have students sign sentences from Part E, Lesson 5.
3. Share homework from Lesson 5.

INTRODUCE NEW SIGNS

Special Note: **-ly Marker**.

To form adverbs and other **-ly** ending words, simply: (1) sign the base word, and immediately (2) use this ending marker.

Nouns	Verbs	Adjectives	Adverbs
basketball	1. Regular	all	together
dance	hurry	loud	
football	kick	quiet	
game	like		
movie	pick		
puzzle	pull		
swim	push		
	roll		
ball	2. Irregular		
balloon	blow		
bat	bring		
bicycle	catch		
doll	fall		
drum	give		
horn	ride		
kite	swim		
rope	throw		
skate			
toy			
wagon			

EXERCISE

1. Go over vocabulary words twice.
2. Students can practice in small groups.
3. Sign words to students. Students tell what they are.

SENTENCES

1. Roll the ball to Karen.
2. I like to jump rope.
3. The drum and horn are loud.
4. I want to go dancing.
5. Pick up all the games, please.
6. Can you throw and catch the ball?
7. The boys pushed the wagon.
8. All the girls pulled on the rope.
9. Who can swim quietly?
10. I like to ride my bicycle slowly.
11. The kite fell out of the tree.

12. Hurry and pick up your toys.
13. The boys and girls played a game quietly together.
14. I will kick the football. You will catch it.

ASSIGNMENT POSSIBILITIES

1. Be prepared to sign the sentences in Part E.
2. Be prepared to sign a paragraph with at least three sentences, telling about yourself.

VOCABULARY

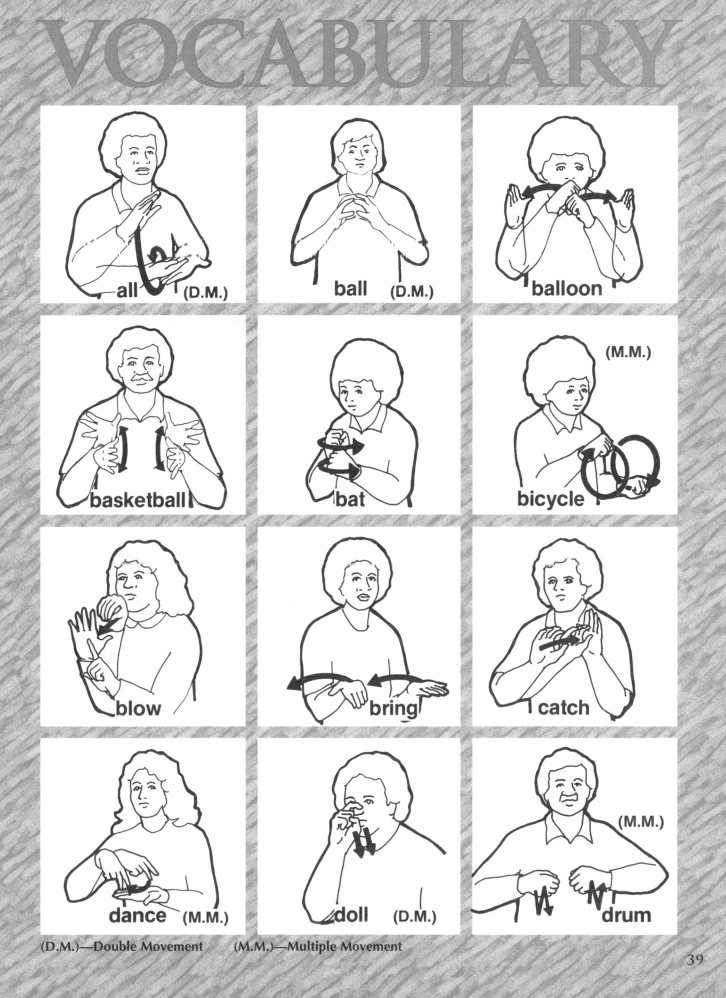

all (D.M.)

ball (D.M.)

balloon

basketball

bat

bicycle (M.M.)

blow

bring

catch

dance (M.M.)

doll (D.M.)

drum (M.M.)

(D.M.)—Double Movement   (M.M.)—Multiple Movement

39

fall (v)

football

game

give

hide

horn

hurry

kick

kite

like

loud (D.M.)

movie (M.M.)

pick

pull

push

puzzle

quiet

ride

roll (D.M.)

rope

alternating movement

skate (M.M.)

swim (D.M.)

throw

together

41

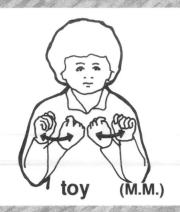

toy (M.M.)

wagon

7 FOOD

FINGER SPELLING GAME

Words that Sound Alike. (homonyms)

Prepare a list of words that sound the same, but are spelled differently. Finger spell, for instance, *'one.'* Ask students to interpret the finger spelling and volunteer to finger spell the word that sounds the same, *'won.'*

One person can remain the leader or the correct volunteer can choose from the prepared list for the next round.

To start your list: son/sun; by/buy; two/to/too; ate/eight; here/hear; so/sew; be/bee; for/four; red/read; write/right; beet/beat.

REVIEW

1. Review Lesson 6 signs and any others that have been difficult.
2. Sign the sentences from Part E, Lesson 6.
3. Share homework assignment from Lesson 6.
4. Review **-ly Markers**. Sign to be interpreted:

beautifully	fatherly	newly
slowly	motherly	openly
loudly	womanly	timely
quietly	manly	timely

INTRODUCE NEW SIGNS

Nouns	cracker	ice cream	**Adjectives**
breakfast	egg	pop	careful
lunch	jelly	popcorn	cold
dinner	juice		hot
fruit	milk	**Verbs**	warm
apple	peanut butter	1. Regular	full
banana	potato	cook	hungry
grape	salad	pass	thirsty
pear	sandwich	pour	
bread	fish	smell	**Adverbs**
butter	meat	2. Irregular	after
cheese	hamburger	eat	before
cookie	hot dog	drink	almost
		make	now
			maybe

EXERCISE

1. Go over vocabulary words twice.
2. Students can practice in small groups.
3. Sign words to students. Students tell what they are.

SENTENCES

1. My family likes to make popcorn.
2. It is time to eat breakfast.
3. I want cookies and milk, please.
4. Father is cooking dinner.
5. Mother wants me to eat carrots.
6. Please pass the potatoes and fish.
7. We will have eggs, bread, butter, and juice.
8. I want a peanut butter and jelly sandwich.
9. We are having hamburgers, cheese, and pop for dinner.
10. The boys made a fruit salad with bananas, grapes, pears, and apples.
11. He walked slowly home and cooked dinner for his mother and father.
12. Maybe they will watch television after dinner.
13. Have a full glass of milk with your crackers and banana.
14. I smell meat cooking. Is it hamburgers or hot dogs?
15. Who is thirsty? Do you want fruit juice or milk?

ASSIGNMENT POSSIBILITIES

1. Be prepared to sign sentences in Part E.
2. Create a short dialogue with a partner and be prepared to sign it.

VOCABULARY

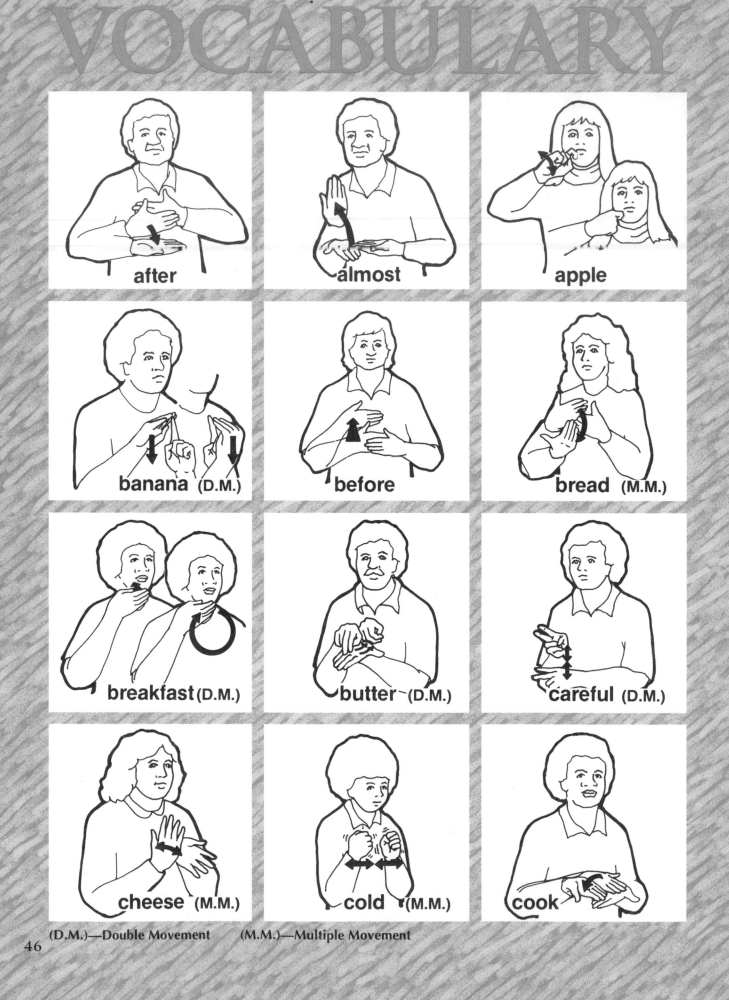

after

almost

apple

banana (D.M.)

before

bread (M.M.)

breakfast (D.M.)

butter (D.M.)

careful (D.M.)

cheese (M.M.)

cold (M.M.)

cook

(D.M.)—Double Movement   (M.M.)—Multiple Movement

cookie

cracker (D.M.)

dinner (D.M.)

drink

eat (D.M.)

egg (D.M.)

fish

fruit

full

grape (M.M.)

hamburger

hot

47

hot dog

hungry

ice cream (D.M.)

jelly

juice

lunch (D.M.)

make

maybe (M.M.)

meat (M.M.)

milk (M.M.)

now

pass

48

peanut butter

pear

pop

popcorn (M.M.)

potato (D.M.)

pour

salad (M.M.)

sandwich

smell

thirsty

warm

49

8 DOMESTIC ANIMALS

SIGNING/ FINGER SPELLING GAME

I'm Going to the Store.

"I'm going to the store and I'm going to buy _____(sign/finger spell)."

The item can be finger spelled, but encourage signs. Three or four small groups work well. If a child forgets what item has been previously added to the list, they drop out.

REVIEW

1. Review signs from Lesson 7 and any other signs that have been difficult.
2. Sign sentences from Part E, Lesson 7.
3. Share homework assignment from Lesson 7.

INTRODUCE NEW SIGNS

Nouns		**Verbs**	**Prepositions**
animal	pig	1. Regular	around
cat, kitten	rabbit	brush	between
chicken	sheep	carry	from
cow	turkey	2. Irregular	
dog, puppy	turtle	feed	**Adverb**
duck		forgot	not
goat	farm	grow	
hamster	farmer	know	**Question Words**
horse	barn	sing	when
mouse	cage		which

EXERCISES

1. Go over vocabulary words twice.
2. Students can practice in small groups.
3. Sign words to students. Students tell what they are.

SENTENCES

1. I have a new horse.
2. The cat sat on the chair.
3. Walk the cow around the barn.
4. Please feed the chickens and the ducks.
5. Do not forget to put the hamster in the big, brown cage.
6. The pig is very dirty. Be careful when you feed it.
7. The rabbits jumped around the cage.
8. When will the cat catch the mouse?
9. The duck swam in the water.
10. Kathy got eggs from the chickens.
11. My puppies like to run between the barn and the house.

ASSIGNMENT POSSIBILITIES

1. Be prepared to sign the sentences in Part E.
2. Prepare a short joke or riddle to be finger spelled/signed.

VOCABULARY

animal (D.M.)

around

barn

between (M.M.)

bird (D.M.)

brush (D.M.)

cage

carry

cat

chicken

cow

dog

(D.M.)—Double Movement   (M.M.)—Multiple Movement

54

duck

farm

farmer

feed

forget

from

goat

grow

hamster

horse

kitten

know

55

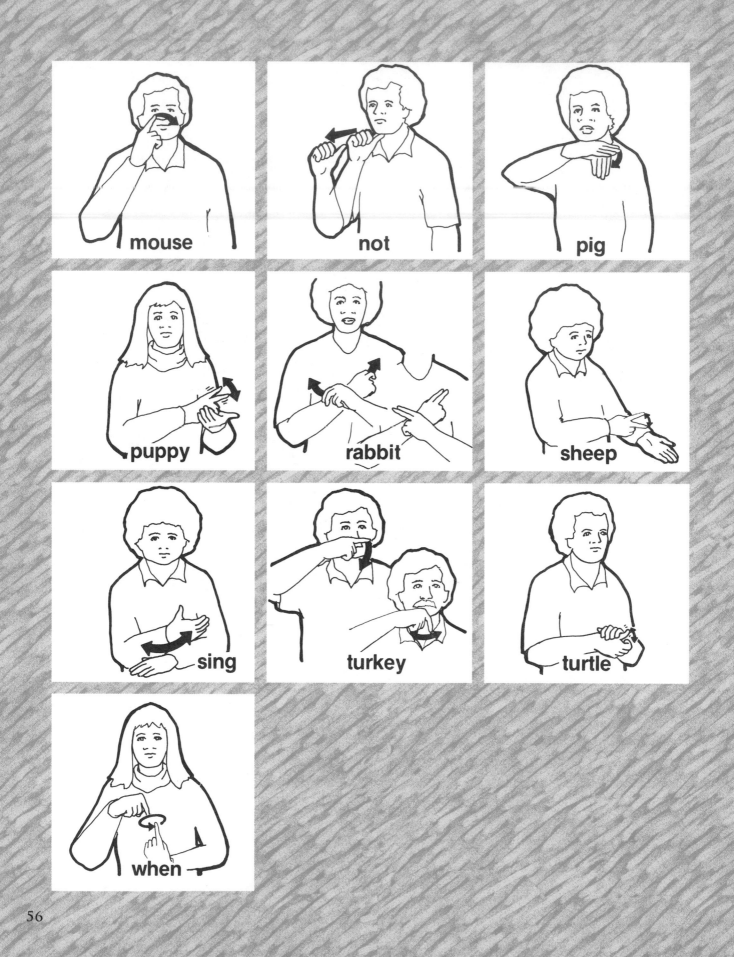

 WILD ANIMALS

FINGER SPELLING/SIGN GAME

Things That Go Together

Prepare a list of words that are associated as pairs. Use vocabulary words when possible: ice cream/cake; bread/butter; cheese/crackers; boy/girl; cat/dog; peanut butter/jelly; hot/cold; mother/father; meat/potatoes; red, white/blue; paper/pencil.

The first word is signed or finger spelled. A volunteer completes the match.

REVIEW

1. Review signs from Lesson 8 and any other signs that have been difficult.
2. Sign sentences from Part E, Lesson 8.
3. Share homework assignment from Lesson 8.
4. Review irregular **past tense verbs**. How would you sign:

knew	ate	caught	hid
sang	drank	fell	broke
grew	made	gave	got
forgot	blew	rode	went

INTRODUCE NEW SIGNS

Nouns		**Verbs**	**Adjectives**
alligator	owl	1. Regular	afraid
bear	raccoon	chase	large
bee	snake	crawl	scary
bug	spider	follow	tall
butterfly	squirrel	2. Irregular	ugly
deer	tiger	fly	
elephant	wolf		
fox	zebra		
frog	jungle		
giraffe	place		
lion	thing		
monkey	woods		

EXERCISES

1 Go over vocabulary words twice.
2 Students can practice in small groups.
3 Sign words to students. Students tell what they are.

SENTENCES

1. The giraffe is very tall.
2. I am afraid of snakes.
3. The owl ate the bug.
4. The lion chased the deer.
5. The squirrel sat quietly on the fence.
6. The raccoon washed the fish.
7. Look at the frog jump.
8. The ugly spider crawled up the chair.
9. The monkey crawled down the tree to the bananas.
10. The wolf was following the zebra.
11. The jungle is a very scary place to walk.
12. The alligator caught and ate the butterfly.

ASSIGNMENT POSSIBILITIES

1. Be prepared to sign the sentences in Part E.
2. Be prepared to sign a short story about a pet you have or an animal you know about. The story must have at least three sentences.

VOCABULARY

afraid

alligator

bear

bee

bug

butterfly

chase

crawl

deer

elephant

fly (M.M.)

follow

(D.M.)—Double Movement   (M.M.)—Multiple Movement

fox

frog

giraffe

jungle (D.M.)

large

lion

monkey

owl

place

raccoon

scary

snake

61

spider

squirrel

thing

tiger

ugly

wolf

(D.M.)

woods

zebra

10 TRANSPORTATION

FINGER SPELLING/ SIGN GAMES

(Choose One)

1. Words and Proper Names

Finger spell names of streets in your town, spelling words, names of parents or siblings.

2. Animal Game

Leader speaks or signs "I am thinking of an animal that…"

...is tall. (giraffe)

...has a long tail. (alligator)

...lives in water. (fish)

...washes its food. (raccoon)

...hunts at night. (owl)

A volunteer signs their guess—either a single word answer or an answer prefaced by the signs for "Is it a(n)_____."

Leader can change with correct guesses, or remain the same throughout.

REVIEW

1. Lesson 9 signs and any other signs that have been difficult.
2. Sign sentences from Part E, Lesson 9.
3. Share homework assignment from Lesson 9.

INTRODUCE NEW SIGNS

Nouns	airplane	**Pronouns**	**Verbs**
bus	boat	our	1. Regular
car	helicopter	us	fix
jeep	motorcycle	we	move
taxi	rocket	they	stop
truck	ship	them	2. Irregular
van	train		drive
airport		**Adverb**	see
gas		sometime	take off
station			3. Auxiliary
street		**Preposition**	must
		for	

EXERCISES

1. Go over vocabulary words twice.
2. Students can practice in small groups.
3. Sign words to students. Students tell what they are.

SENTENCES

1. Look at the old helicopter
2. That train is going fast.
3. That train is very long.
4. Our father has a new jeep.
5. Look at that rocket take off.
6. Please help me move your boat.
7. My motorcycle is slow sometimes.
8. The ship will bring many new trucks.
9. They want to watch the airplane take off.
10. Taxis, bicycles, and buses must stop for red lights on the street.
11. Our car stopped. Please help me fix it.
12. We will move the van for them.
13. Fix the car and come home for dinner.
14. The red street light stopped all cars and trucks.
15. We can see a helicopter, airplane, and rocket at the airport.

ASSIGNMENT POSSIBILITIES

1. Be prepared to sign the sentences from Part E.
2. What type of transportation (mode) would you choose to have? Why? Prepare at least three sentences to be signed answering these two questions—be serious or humorous.

VOCABULARY

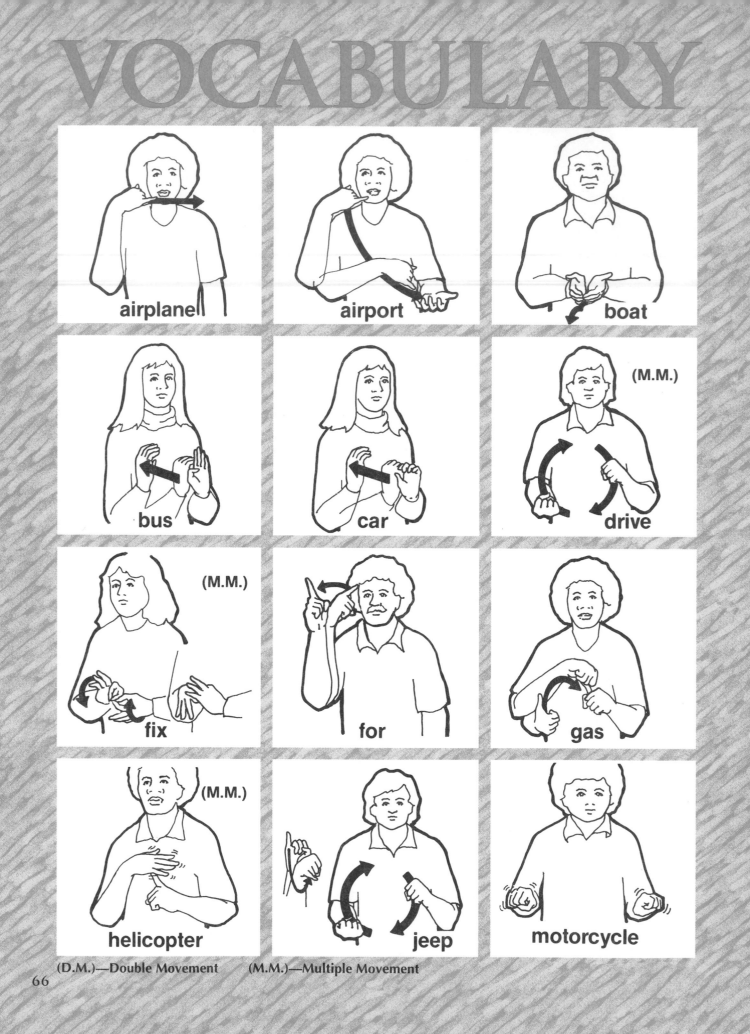

airplane

airport

boat

bus

car

(M.M.) drive

(M.M.) fix

for

gas

(M.M.) helicopter

jeep

motorcycle

(D.M.)—Double Movement   (M.M.)—Multiple Movement

move

must

our

rocket

see

ship

sometime

station

stop

street

take

take off

taxi

them

they

train

truck

us

van

we

11 NATURE

SIGNING GAMES

(Choose One)

1. Last Letter Continuation.
Leader signs a word, or finger spells a word, then points to someone to continue. That person must sign or finger spell a word that begins with the last letter of the leader's word.

For example, if the leader signs *'jeep,'* the next designated person would sign a word beginning with 'p.'

Signs or finger spelling can be at random or in conformity with categories (foods, vegetables, animals).

2. Read A Sign, Finger Spell It Back.
Leader presents a sign, for example *'home.'* A chosen or designated person finger spells *'h-o-m-e.'*

REVIEW

1. Lesson 10 signs and any other signs that have been difficult.
2. Sign sentences from Part E, Lesson 10.
3. Share homework assignments from Lesson 10.

INTRODUCE NEW SIGNS

Special Note: **-y Markers**

To add a **y**, commonly to nouns (wind/windy, ice/icy): (1) sign the base word, and immediately (2) add this sign marker:

Nouns		sun	Adjectives
day	night	tree	bright
fire	ocean	wind	hard
fog	park		high
forest	rain	**Verbs**	soft
grass	rainbow	1. Regular	
ice	river	camp	**Adverb**
lake	rock	hike	once
and	sky	2. Irregular	
leaf	snow	dig	**Preposition**
moon	star	feel	through

EXERCISES

1. Go over vocabulary words twice.
2. Students can practice in small groups.
3. Sign words to students. Students tell what they are.

SENTENCES

1. The rock is hard.
2. We like to hike through the trees.
3. Billy will swim in the river.
4. They saw a rainbow after the rain.
5. I see the sun in the day and before it gets warm.
6. The stars and the moon come out at night.
7. The rain helped put the fire out.
8. I love to watch the snow and the wind.
9. It was very foggy at the ocean.
10. The sun was very bright on the mountains.
11. I sat in the grass and watched the leaves fall.
12. The rain feels soft falling from the sky.
13. They are going camping in the forest. We are going with them.
14. The park has green and grassy mountains.
15. You can see a beautiful rainbow after a rain.

ASSIGNMENT POSSIBILITIES

1. Be prepared to sign sentences from Part E.
2. Prepare an ending with at least three sentences to this starting phrase:
   "Once upon a time a little ...." Be prepared to sign the entire story.

VOCABULARY

bright

camp

day

dig

feel

fire (M.M.)

fog

forest (D.M.)

grass

hard

high

hike (D.M.)

(D.M.)—Double Movement   (M.M.)—Multiple Movement

72

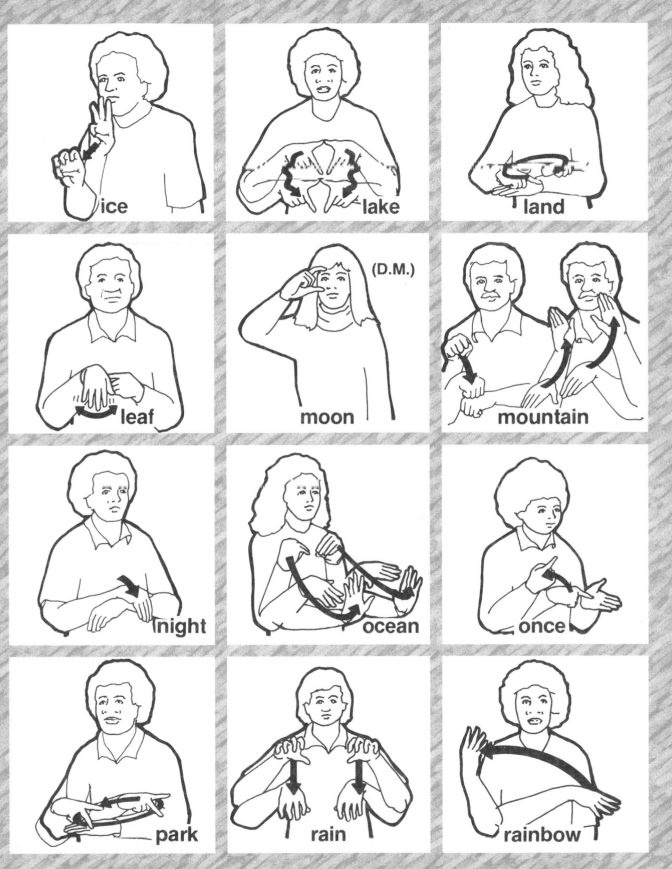

ice

lake

land

leaf

moon (D.M.)

mountain

night

ocean

once

park

rain

rainbow

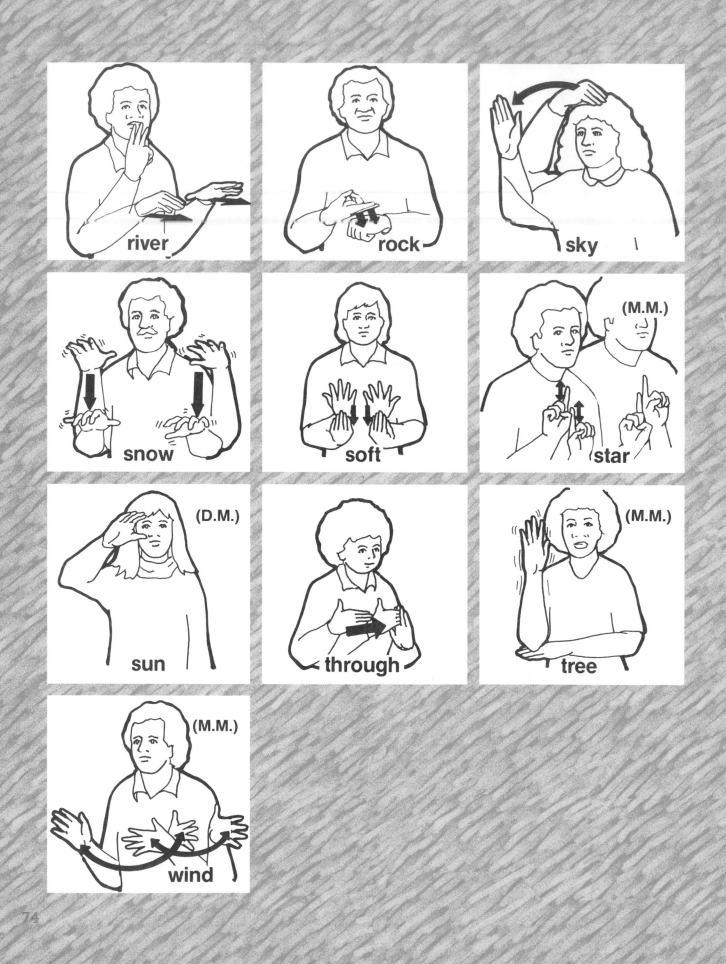

river

rock

sky

snow

soft

star (M.M.)

sun (D.M.)

through

tree (M.M.)

wind (M.M.)

74

12 OCCUPATIONS

SIGNING GAME

What (or Who) Am I?—Number 1

Leader thinks of a tangible object, then signs clues—for instance, its size, color, or use. Several clues should be presented before the leader encourages volunteers to guess.

The exchanges should be through signs, supplemented by finger spelling.

Use past vocabulary words for the objects to be guessed.

After initial clues, further clues should be presented as needed.

REVIEW

1. Review Lesson 11 signs and any other signs that have been difficult.
2. Sign sentences from Part E, Lesson 11.
3. Share homework assignments from Lesson 11.
4. Review **-y marker** endings.

Either: (a) sign the following words for students to interpret, (b) speak them for student signing, or (c) finger spell them for volunteers to sign or verbally identify:

sleepy	meaty	smelly
fruity	foggy	rocky
juicy	windy	grassy
milky	sunny	buggy
		brushy

To keep the students alert, intersperse these words. They are words that normally have **y** ending sounds:

cookie	family	monkey
carry	hurry	story
dirty	jelly	turkey

INTRODUCE NEW SIGNS

Special Note: **Person Concept.**

Often occupations use a compound sign. This sign is person:

It commonly follows words such as: mail, police, fire, or garbage to form mail person, police person, etc. The person sign need not differentiate sex.

Nouns		Verbs	Adjectives
bus	restaurant	1. Regular	as
driver	store	dream	front
cowboy		remember	
doctor		wait	**Prepositions**
fire person		work	behind
garbage person		2. Irregular	near
mail person		buy	
nurse police		meet	
person		sell	
building		send	
fire station		steal	
hospital		sweep	
letter		tell	
office			

EXERCISE

1. Go over vocabulary words twice.
2. Students can practice in small groups.
3. Sign words to students. Students tell what they are.

SENTENCES

1. Wait for the garbage person.
2. The mail person brings me letters.
3. I will buy the apples at the store.
4. The doctor and nurse work at the hospital.
5. The police person caught the man who stole my bicycle.
6. Many people dream of being a cowboy.
7. Tell the fire person where the fire is.
8. Remember to go to the hospital to meet your brother and sister.
9. Please send Kathy to the restaurant when she comes home.
10. Sweep the office before you send the letter to the hospital.
11. I am sleepy when I get up to go to school.
12. I hardly saw him. He ran through the windy street very quickly.
13. The fire station is a red building with trees near it.
14. The office building is newly painted.
15. Remember! Work on the car before you play football.

ASSIGNMENT POSSIBILITIES

1. Be prepared to sign sentences from Part E.
2. Be prepared to describe an occupation—an occupation for which you have learned a sign, or make up your own sign.

Your description should be at least three sentences long.

VOCABULARY

as

behind

building

bus driver

buy

cowboy

doctor (D.M.)

dream

fire person (M.M.)

fire station (M.M.)

front

garbage person

(D.M.)—Double Movement   (M.M.)—Multiple Movement

hospital

letter

mail person

meet

near

nurse (D.M.)

office

police person

remember

restaurant

sell

send

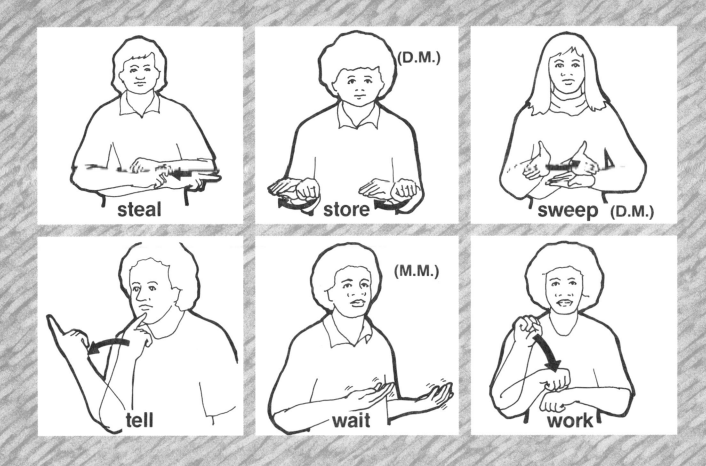

steal

store (D.M.)

sweep (D.M.)

tell

wait (M.M.)

work

13 EMOTIONS

SIGNING GAME

What (or Who) Am I?—Number 2

Leader chooses an object or occupation. Volunteers, through signing, ask questions to which the leader can only answer 'yes' or 'no.' This requires all students to read the signing of all previous questions, so that future questions are relevant and zero in on the leader's object or occupation.

Simple questions by volunteers can be prefaced by: "Are you...(insert: size, color, use, living, etc.)."

REVIEW

1. Lesson 12 signs and any other signs that have been difficult.
2. Sign sentences from Part E, Lesson 12.
3. Share homework assignment from Lesson 12.
4. Review **past tense** and **-ly markers.**
   Sign or have volunteers sign:

   > newly made
   > quickly forgot
   > slowly carried
   > carefully wrote

INTRODUCE NEW SIGNS

Adjectives-Emotions	lazy	**Verbs**	2. Irregular
angry	lonely	1. Regular	lose
bad	mad	die	think
fine	sad	enjoy	win
funny	silly	excite	3. Auxiliary
good	sorry	hug	may
happy	tired	live	
		scream	
		surprise	

EXERCISES

1. Go over vocabulary words twice.
2. Students can practice in small groups.
3. Sign words to students. Students tell what they are.

SENTENCES

1. I enjoy winning.
2. You are silly.
3. The little girl feels lonely.
4. The boy may be afraid of the lazy dog.
5. May I have a drink? I am thirsty.
6. I was sad when my cat died.
7. He is excited that he is going to the ocean.
8. I love to be lazy sometimes.
9. I am sorry that I forgot to stop at the store.
10. Kathy was surprised when Gabriel gave her a dog.
11. I am mad and feel like screaming.
12. Maybe you think you are funny.
13. Happy people make me feel good.
14. The small girl hugged her orange and white kitten.
15. I live near a large lake where I can fish when I want.

ASSIGNMENT POSSIBILITIES

1. Be prepared to sign sentences from Part E.
2. Complete this sentence, adding at least two others in explanation:

I feel _____ when _____.

VOCABULARY

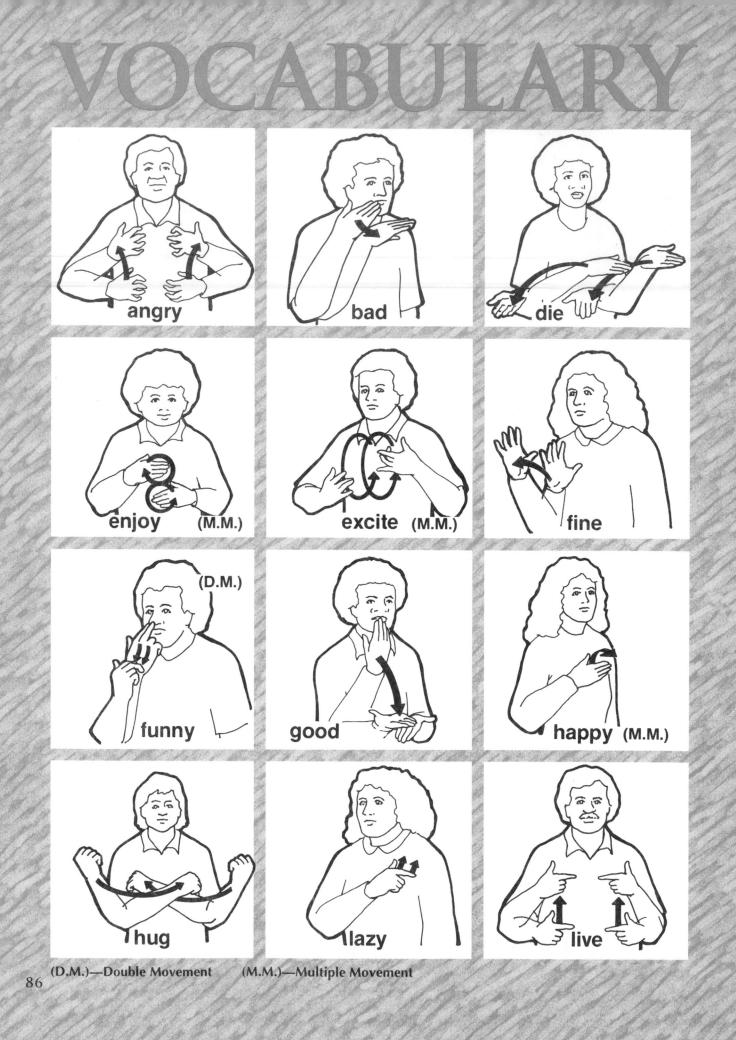

angry

bad

die

enjoy (M.M.)

excite (M.M.)

fine

funny (D.M.)

good

happy (M.M.)

hug

lazy

live

(D.M.)—Double Movement   (M.M.)—Multiple Movement

lonely

lose

mad

may

sad

scream

silly (D.M.)

sorry

surprise

think

tired

win

14 TIME

SIGNING GAME

(Choose One)

1. **Building a Story**

   A designated person begins by signing, or finger spelling, a single word. In a random or established order, subsequent words are added one at a time to build sentences and a story.

   All preceding words should be signed before a new word is added. If this proves too difficult, at least repeat the immediate sentence until it is complete.

2. **Vocabulary Review**

   Leader states a category—color, occupation, food, animal, transportation—and signs, or finger spells, something from that category. Leader establishesan order of rotation.

   Each player adds, through signing or finger spelling, something different to the stated category.

   Game should be paced. Participants must be attentive to past category examples, as examples can be used only once per category.

REVIEW

1. Lesson 13 signs and any other signs that have been difficult.
2. Sign sentences from Part E, Lesson 13.
3. Share homework assignment from Lesson 13.
4. Review **past tense**.

   Leader signs for interpretation, or leader asks for volunteers to sign:

forgot	lived	smelled	felt
won	met	dug	swept
excited	send	swam	remembered
picked	told	hiked	camped

INTRODUCE NEW SIGNS

Months	Days	Seasons	Time
January	Monday	summer	today
February	Tuesday	spring	morning
March	Wednesday	winter	afternoon
April	Thursday	fall	evening
May	Friday		tomorrow
June	Saturday		yesterday
July	Sunday		minute
August			hour
September			week
October			month
November			year
December			o'clock
			next

EXERCISES

1. Go over vocabulary words twice.
2. Students can practice in small groups.
3. Sign words to students. Students tell what they are.

SENTENCES

1. Tomorrow will be Wednesday.
2. Friday is the last day of school.
3. December, January, and February are winter months.
4. March, April, and May are spring months.
5. June, July, and August are summer months.
6. September, October, and November are fall months.
7. The days of the week are Monday, Tuesday, Wednesday, Thursday, Friday, Saturday, and Sunday.
8. Yesterday I happily went for a walk in the park.
9. Tomorrow afternoon we will go to see the animals.
10. In the spring, our school is out in May.
11. Yesterday afternoon we went to the store to buy new shoes.
12. My mother and father painted our house a bright blue this summer.
13. Saturday and Sunday are days to sleep in before going to work on Monday.
14. Before you go home on Friday, will you fix the car?
15. This morning the wind felt like cold, cold ice.

ASSIGNMENT POSSIBILITIES

1. Be prepared to sign sentences from Part E.
2. Complete these two sentences, adding—in any order—two other sentences:

   Yesterday I _____. Tomorrow I will _____.

   Be prepared to sign your four sentences.

VOCABULARY

afternoon

April

August

December

evening

fall (n)

February

Friday

hour

January

July

June

(D.M.)—Double Movement   (M.M.)—Multiple Movement

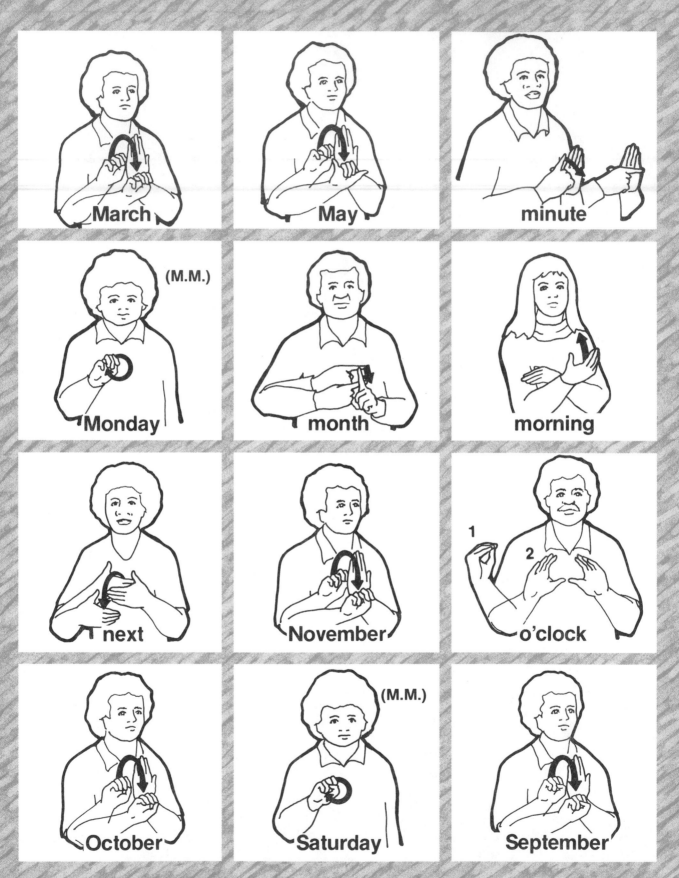

March

May

minute

Monday (M.M.)

month

morning

next

November

o'clock

October

Saturday (M.M.)

September

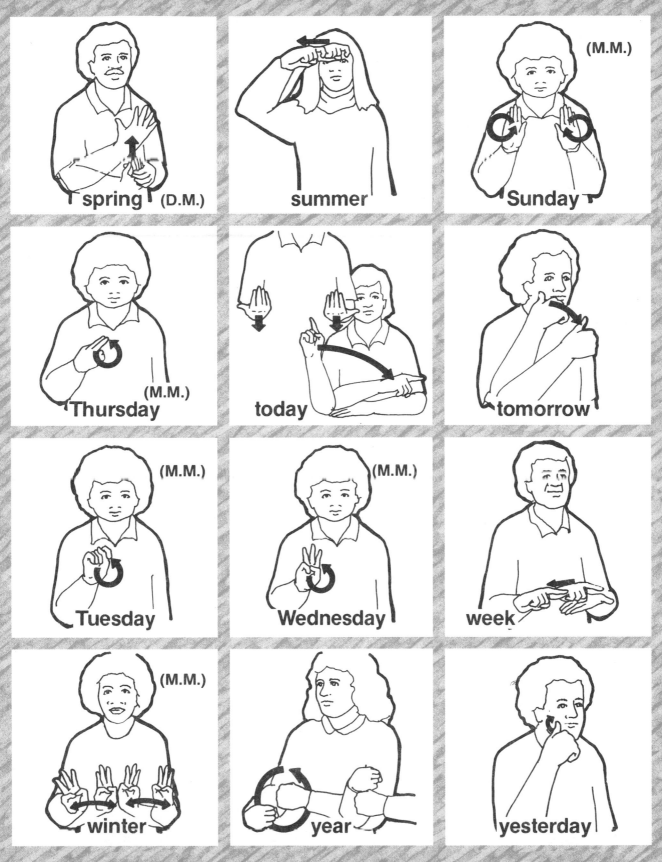

spring (D.M.)

summer

Sunday (M.M.)

Thursday (M.M.)

today

tomorrow

Tuesday (M.M.)

Wednesday (M.M.)

week

winter (M.M.)

year

yesterday

15 CLOTHING

SIGNING GAMES

Analogies

Prepare a list of analogies, such as: *'hot' is* to *'cold,'* as *'in' is* to *'out.'* Use vocabulary words from past lessons.

Leader signs or finger spells only three of the four analogy parts: *'Hot' is* to *'cold,'* as *'in' is* to . A volunteer completes the analogy with a sign or finger spelling.

Here are a few, complete analogies for your list.

up-down/live-die
big-long/little-short
silly-funny/mad-angry
January-December/Monday-Sunday
minute-hour/week-month

fast-slow/black-white
soft-hard/happy-sad
come-go/run-walk
monkey-banana/peanut-elephant
alligator-water/bird-sky

REVIEW

1. Lesson 14 signs and any other signs that have been difficult.
2. Sign sentences from Part E, Lesson 14.
3. Share homework assignment from Lesson 14.

INTRODUCE NEW SIGNS

Nouns		**Verbs**	**Adjectives**
bathrobe	pants	1. Regular	dry
belt	shirt	stay	pretty
blouse	shoe	2. Irregular	short
boot	skirt	fit	small
clothes	socks	keep	wet
coat	sweater	wear	
dress	umbrella		**Adverb**
glasses	face		too
hat	hand		
mitten	head		

EXERCISES

1. Go over the vocabulary words twice.
2. Students can practice in small groups.
3. Sign words to students. Students tell what they are.

SENTENCES

1. My shirt is dirty.
2. My shoes do not fit.
3. Put your hat on your head.
4. Your mittens will keep your hands warm.
5. Your pants are almost too small.
6. Karen has a long, pretty dress that she made.
7. They will get wet without your umbrella.
8. My feet stay dry in my boots.
9. Mother had my coat cleaned on Friday.
10. My old bathrobe is too short.
11. Our family stayed warm by wearing winter clothes.
12. Next time tell me the day of the week that you will go for a ride in the airplane.
13. I will have eggs, a banana, and milk for breakfast, please.
14. The new shirt was too small and the new pants too large.
15. You will not need the umbrella. The sun is out.

ASSIGNMENT POSSIBILITIES

1. Be prepared to sign sentences from Part E.
2. Create a story with at least four sentences. Omit key words—at least five —words. Know if the omitted words are nouns, verbs, or adjectives. When presenting your story, ask for five words. Insert the appropriate words into your story and sign it.
   Signing is encouraged, finger spelling discouraged.

VOCABULARY

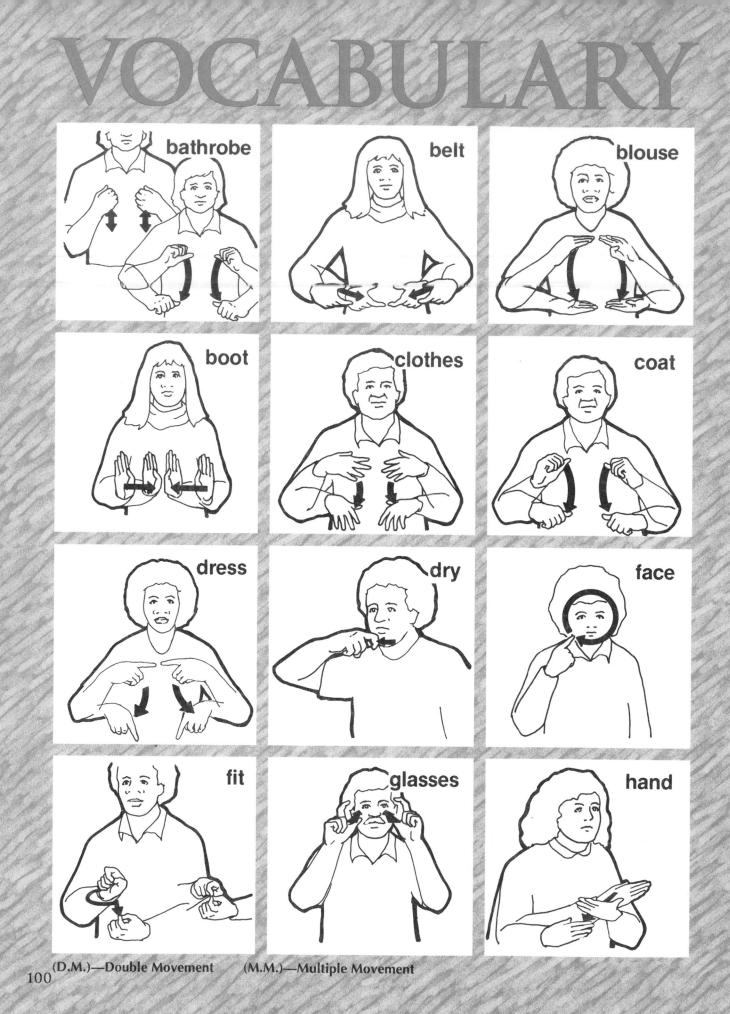

bathrobe

belt

blouse

boot

clothes

coat

dress

dry

face

fit

glasses

hand

(D.M.)—Double Movement   (M.M.)—Multiple Movement

hat

head

keep

mitten

pants

pretty

shirt

shoe

short

skirt

small

socks

stay   sweater   too

umbrella   wear   wet

INDEX